# LEARN TO DRAW... OCEAN WONDERS!

By Mara Conlon

Illustrated by Kerren Barbas Steckler

Designed by Heather Zschock

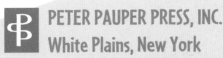 PETER PAUPER PRESS, INC.

White Plains, New York

# For Emily & Jake

### PETER PAUPER PRESS

In 1928, at the age of twenty-two, Peter Beilenson began printing books on a small press in the basement of his parents' home in Larchmont, New York. Peter—and later, his wife, Edna—sought to create fine books that sold at "prices even a pauper could afford."

Today, still family owned and operated, Peter Pauper Press continues to honor our founders' legacy of quality, value, and fun for big kids and small kids alike.

Illustrations copyright © 2015 Kerren Barbas Steckler
Designed by Heather Zschock

Copyright © 2015
Peter Pauper Press, Inc.
Manufactured for Peter Pauper Press, Inc.
202 Mamaroneck Avenue
White Plains, NY 10601
All rights reserved
ISBN 978-1-4413-1604-2
Printed in China

Published in the United Kingdom and Europe by
Peter Pauper Press, Inc. c/o White Pebble International
Unit 2, Plot 11 Terminus Road
Chichester, West Sussex PO19 8TX, UK

7 6 5 4 3 2

Visit us at www.peterpauper.com

## Hey, young artists!

Are you ready to learn how to draw 46 different ocean wonders?
It's easy and fun!
Just follow these steps:

**First,** pick a sea creature you want to draw. (You might want to start with the starfish … it's pretty simple.)

**Next,** trace over the creature with a pencil. This will give you a feel for how to draw the lines.

**Then,** following the numbered boxes, start drawing each new step (shown in red) of the picture in the empty space in each scene, or on a piece of paper.

**Lastly,** if you're an awesome artist (and of course, you are!), try drawing a whole scene with one or more of the sea creatures and things. And remember, don't worry if your drawings look different from the ones in this book—no two ocean wonders are exactly alike!

You're on your way to creating wet, wavy, and scaly masterpieces!

# GET READY! GET SET! DRAW!

# Clownfish

1.

2.

3.

4.

5.

6.

# Angelfish

1.

2.

3.

4.

5.

6.

Draw more like me below!

# Dolphin

1.

2.

3.

4.

5.

6.

# Octopus

1.

2.

3.

4.

5.

6.

# Scallop

1.

2.

3.

4.

5.

6.

# Coral

1.

2.

3.

Trace over me for practice!

# Crab

1.

2.

3.

4.

5.

6.

# Clam

1.

2.

3.

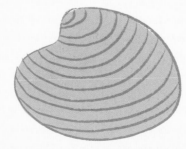

Trace over me
for practice!

# Walrus

1.

2.

3.

4.

5.

6.

# Puffin

1.

2.

3.

4.

5.

6.

# Starfish

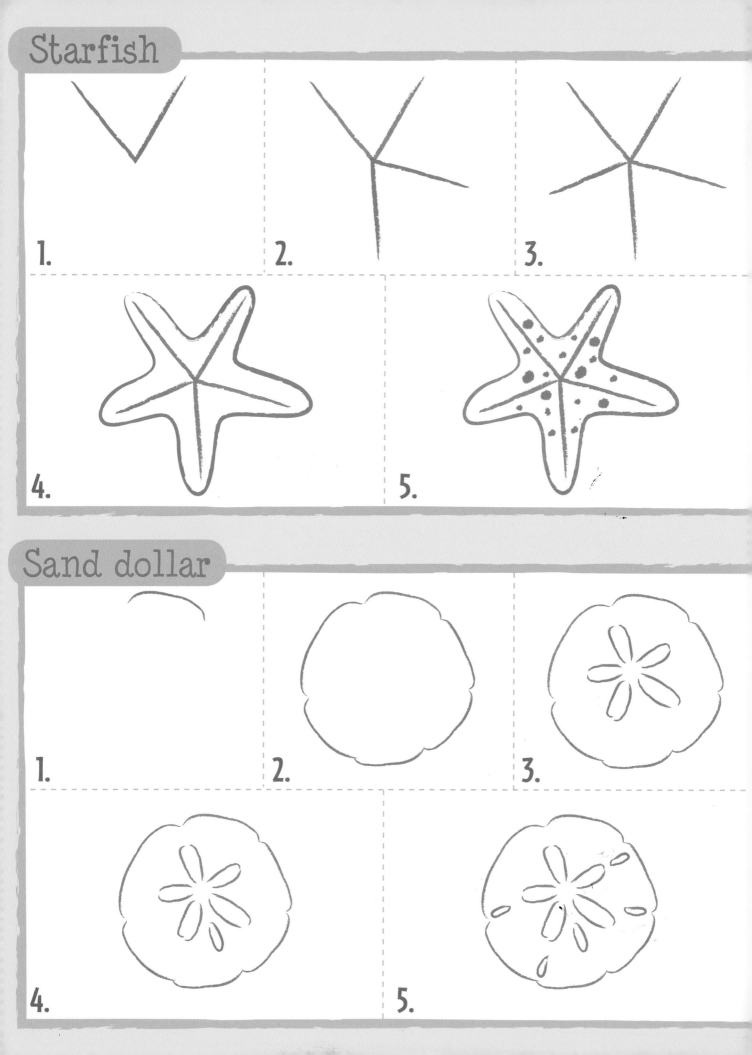

1.
2.
3.
4.
5.

# Sand dollar

1.
2.
3.
4.
5.

# Porcupine fish

1.
2.
3.
4.
5.
6.

# Seagrass

1.
2.
3.
4.

# Seaweed

1.
2.
3.
4.

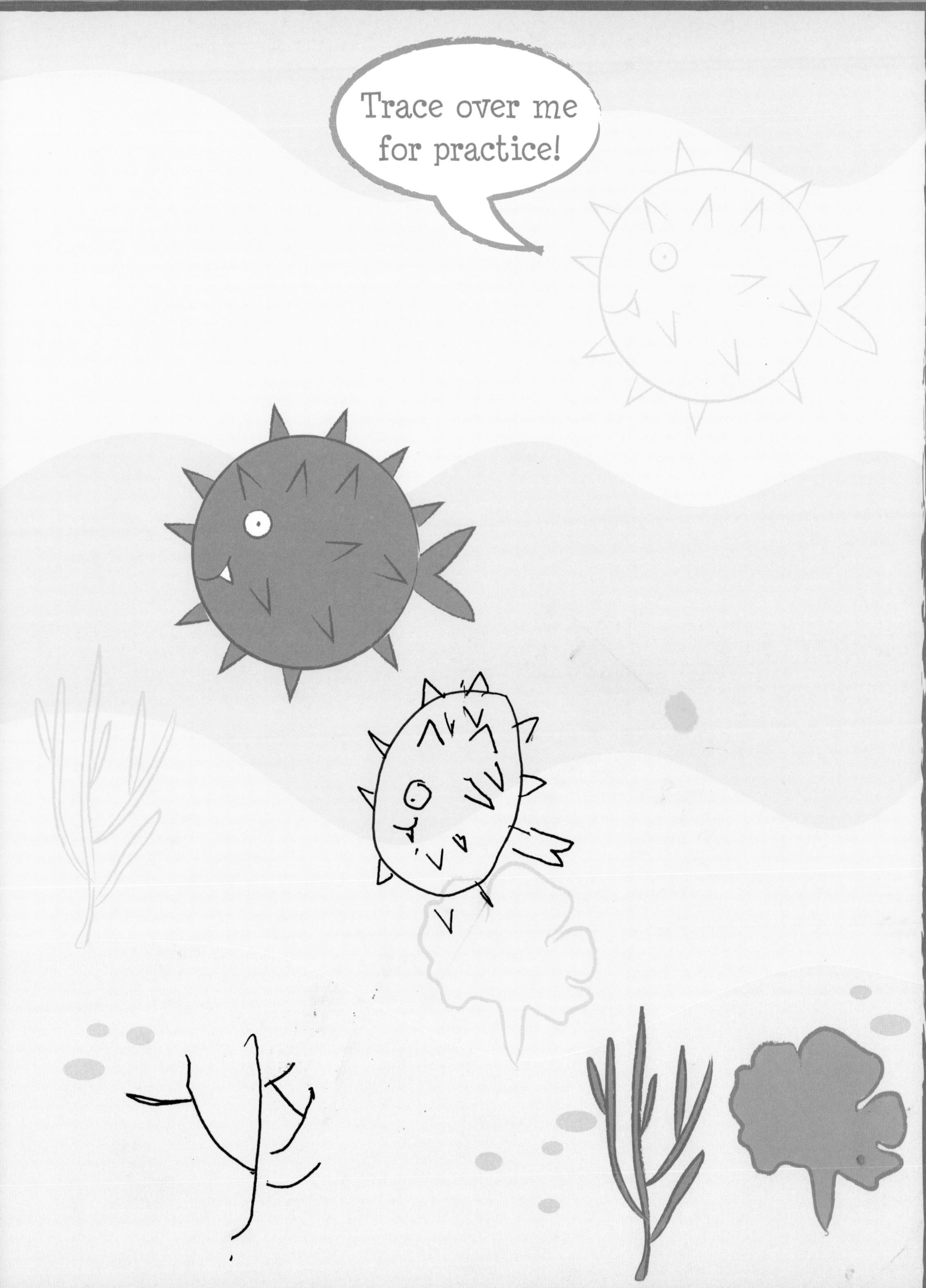
Trace over me
for practice!

# Snail

1.

2.

3.

4.

5.

6.

# Mermaid

1.

2.

3.

4.

5.

6.

# Shark

1.

2.

3.

4.

5.

6.

# Hammerhead shark

1.

2.

3.

4.

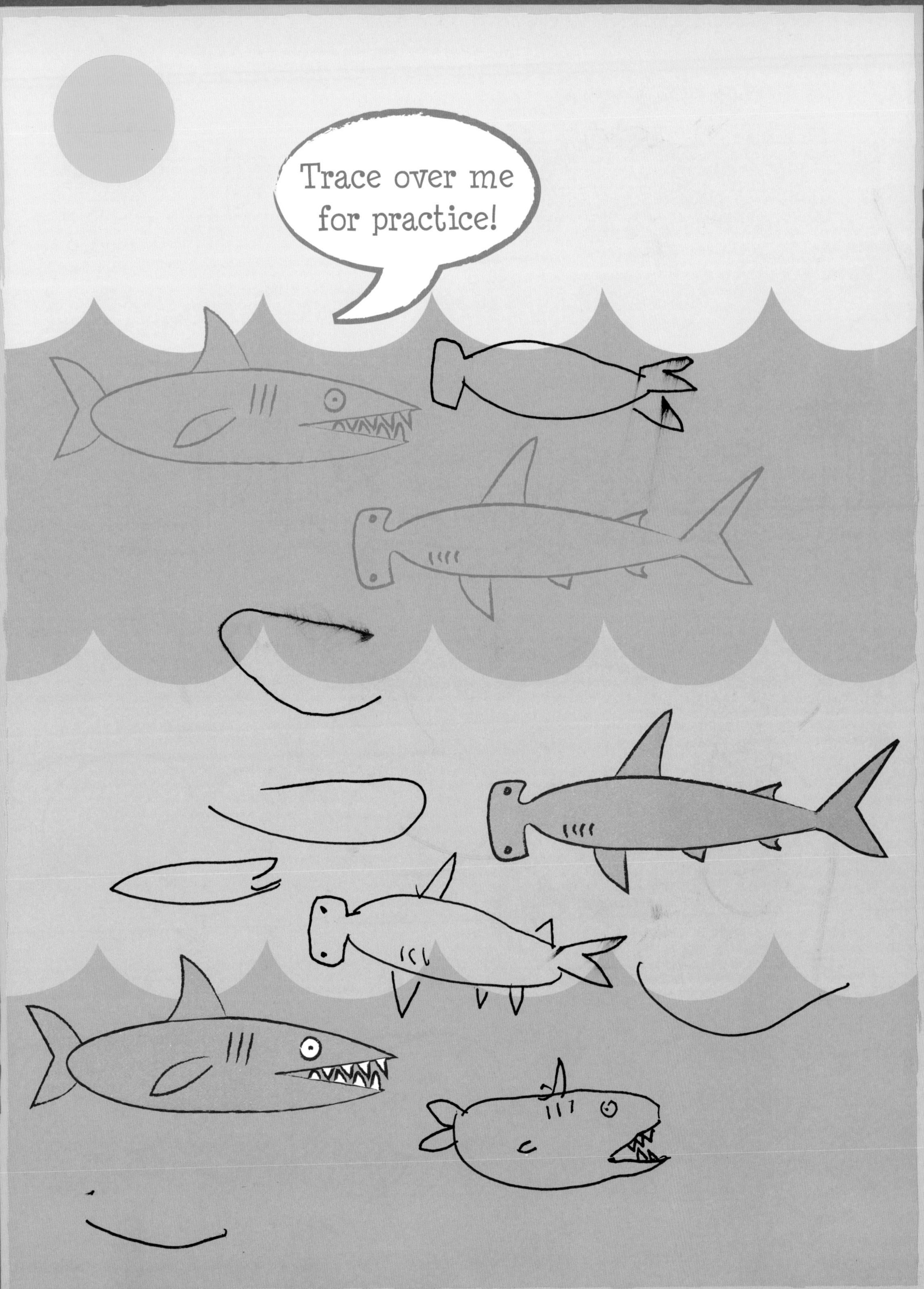
Trace over me for practice!

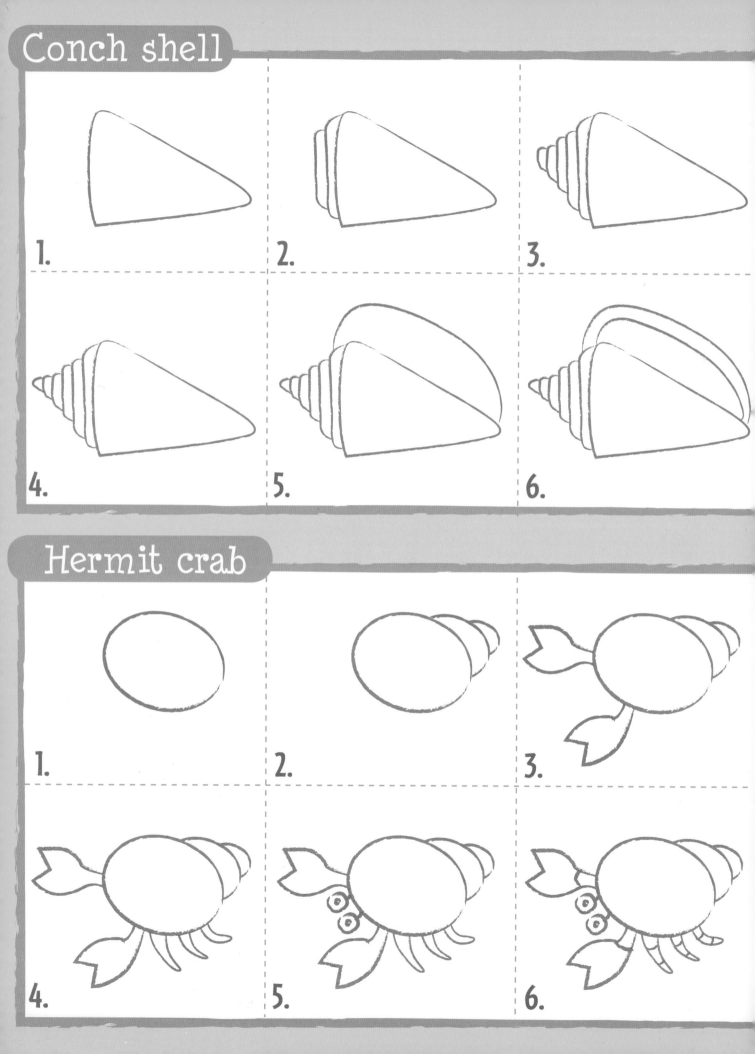

# Conch shell

1.

2.

3.

4.

5.

6.

# Hermit crab

1.

2.

3.

4.

5.

6.

Trace over me
for practice!

# Manta ray

1.

2.

3.

4.

5.

6.

# Swordfish

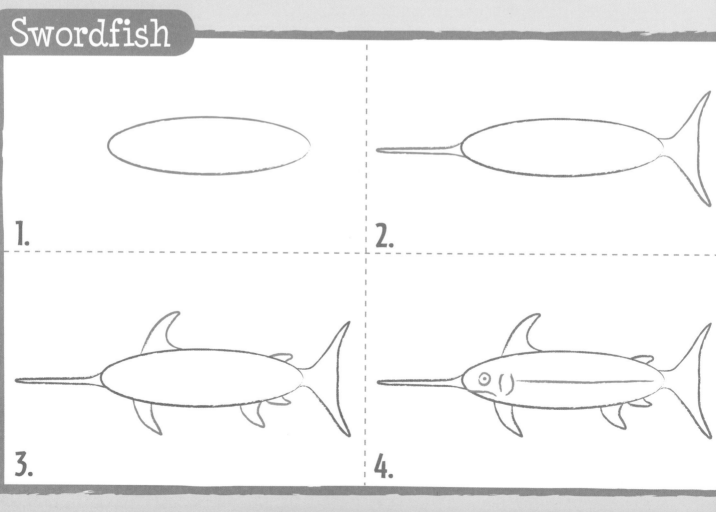

1.

2.

3.

4.

# Orca

1.

2.

3.

4.

5.

6.

# Salmon

1.

2.

3.

4.

## Lobster

1.

2.

3.

4.

5.

6.

## Trap

1.

2.

3.

4.

# Jellyfish

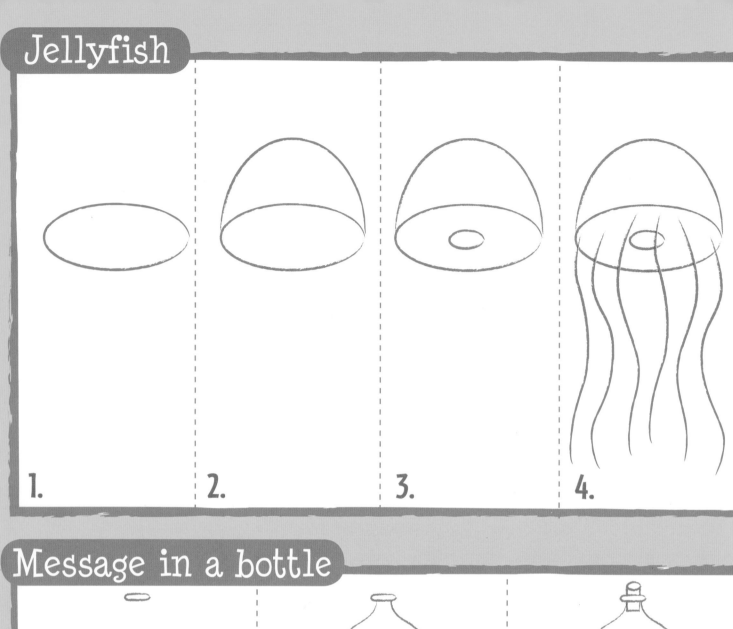

1.    2.    3.    4.

# Message in a bottle

1.    2.    3.

4.    5.    6.

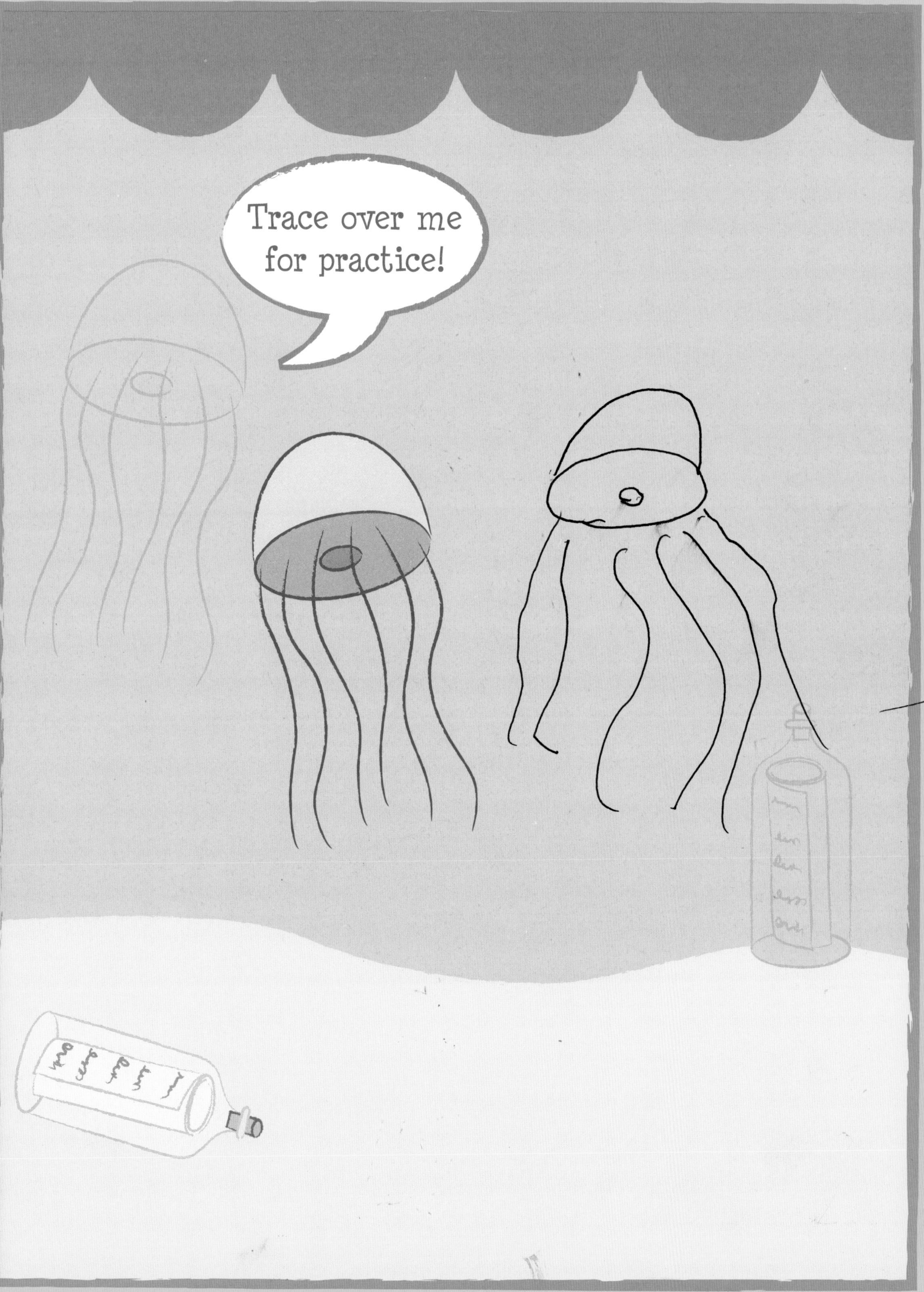
Trace over me for practice!

# Sea turtle

1.

2.

3.

4.

5.

6.

# Eel

1.

2.

3.

4.

5.

6.

# Seahorse

1.

2.

3.

4.

5.

6.

# Horseshoe crab

1.

2.

3.

4.

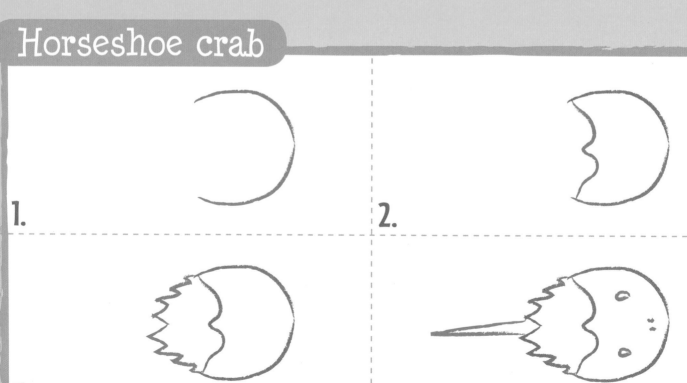

Trace over me for practice!

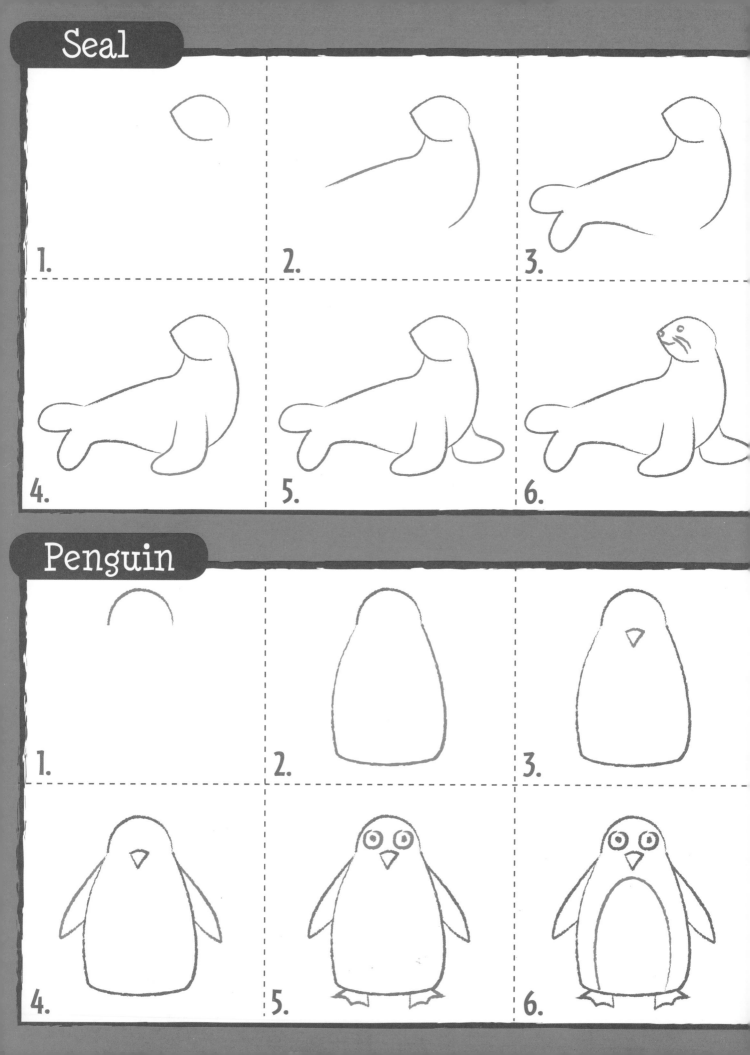

# Seal

1.

2.

3.

4.

5.

6.

# Penguin

1.

2.

3.

4.

5.

6.

# Seagull

1.

2.

3.

4.

5.

6.

# Otter

1.

2.

3.

4.

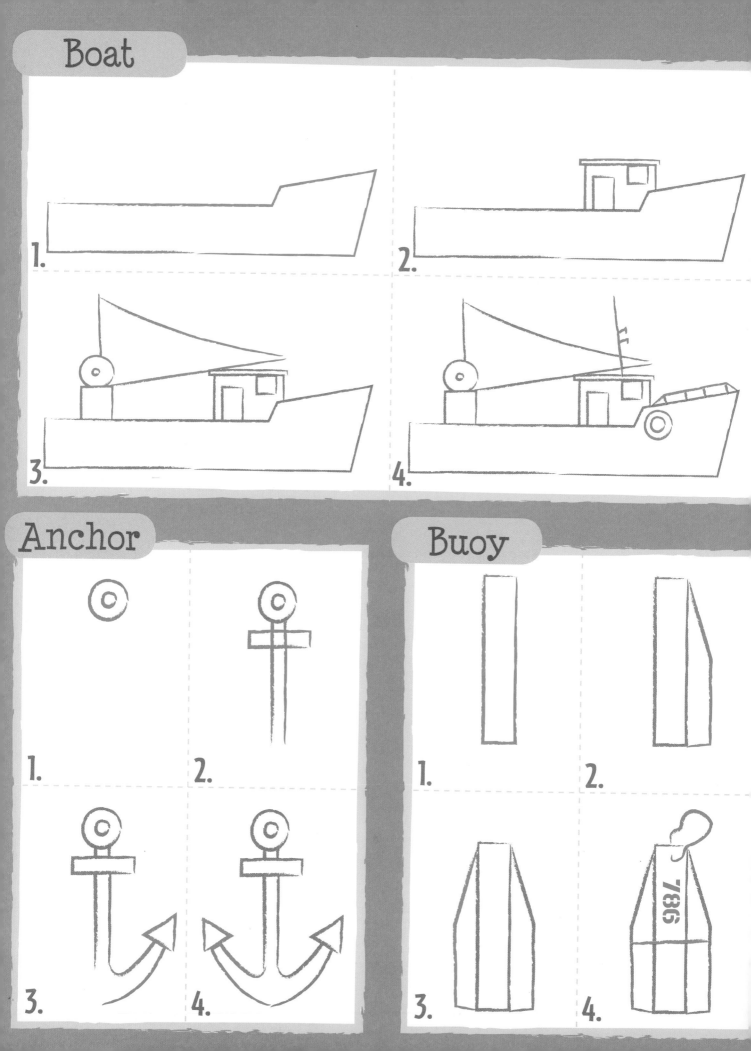

## Boat

1.

2.

3.

4.

## Anchor

1.

2.

3.

4.

## Buoy

1.

2.

3.

4.

# Fishing rod

1.

2.

3.

4.

# Lure

1.

2.

3.

4.

Trace over me for practice!

# Captain

1.

2.

3.

4.

# Lighthouse

1.

2.

3.

4.

# Shipwreck

1.

2.

3.

4.

5.

6.

# Treasure chest

1.

2.

3.

4.

5.

6.

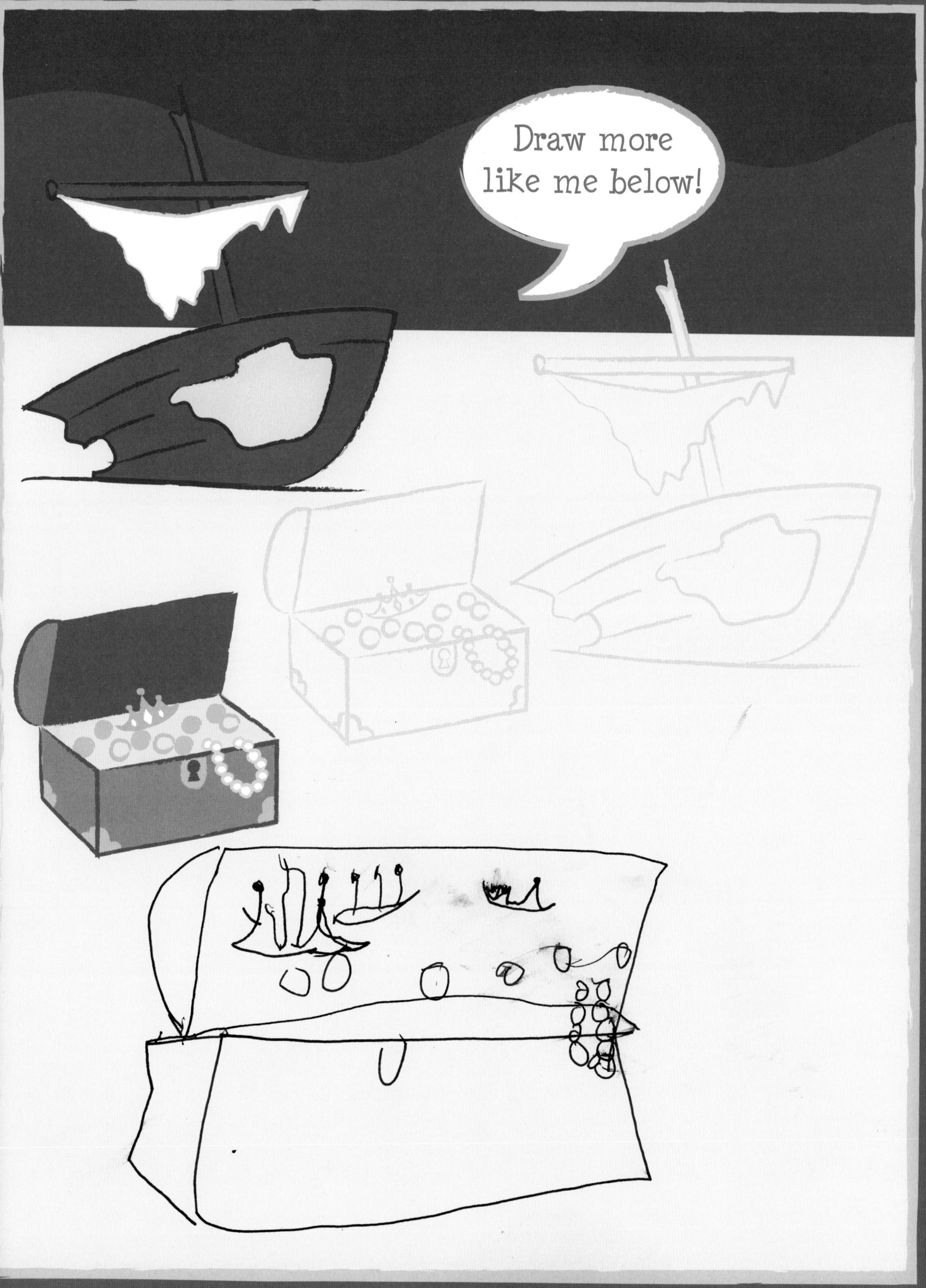
Draw more like me below!

We drew the whole sea.
And now, draw with me!